*Are You Who
You Think You Are?*

A contemplation accompanied by music

Are You Who You Think You Are?

A contemplation accompanied by music

Gabriele

THE WORD
THE UNIVERSAL SPIRIT

First Edition, 2001
Published by:

Gabriele Publishing House
P.O. Box 2221, Deering, NH 03244
(844) 576-0937

WhatsApp/Messenger: +49 151 1883 8742

www.Gabriele-Publishing-House.com

Licensed edition and authorized translation
from the original German title:
"Sind Sie der, für den Sie sich halten?"
Order No. S 332 en

with the consent of
© Verlag DAS WORT GmbH
DER UNIVERSELLE GEIST
LEBEN IM GEISTE GOTTES
Max-Braun-Str. 2
97828 Marktheidenfeld/Altfeld
Germany

The German edition is the work of reference for all
questions regarding the meaning of the contents

ISBN 1-890841-24-2

Introduction

Many people are dissatisfied with their lives and wish that "everything" would be different. Mostly, they have no idea *why* "everything"—the conditions they face in life, their fate—is the way it is, and also have no idea that they themselves have it in their hand to change some things about it. What can be changed? There is only one thing that a person can change: himself—assuming he is willing to recognize himself as the one who he really is.

The message of this little book is: Only the person who recognizes himself can change himself. The person who changes himself toward the good, toward the cosmic law of love which is the only good, his inner quality of living, his character, changes itself, and as a result, the externalities— the course and conditions of his life—can also change accordingly, toward the positive. For each person is the architect of his own fate.

The following explanations, contemplations and exercises offer help from the divine wisdom for self-recognition.

Consciously, we people know—pretty much exactly—who we think we are. Who we really are behind or under the, for the most part, positively arranged façade of daily life lies in our subconscious and in our soul garments. The aspects of our—mostly not so positive—true identity, which consists of the contents of our feelings, of our sensations, of our thinking, speaking and acting, are those energy potentials which are stored in our soul, in our genes, in every cell of our body and in the repository stars of the Fall-cosmos. These radiate, influencing our present life and determining our future as well.

For the one who figures out his shadowed sides, until now kept hidden, and clears them up with the help of the Christ of God and His transforming power, the positive forces of life will become more and more effective during his days on Earth. These forces want to lead and guide each individual person. And toward what? Toward the true life, toward his true self, which is light-filled and pure because it is divine. This spiritual, original being in us, that was hidden from us in the very basis of our soul, waits to be freed. Only we ourselves can unearth this treasure in our innermost being. Self-recognition opens this possibility up to us.

In case recognitions or realizations come up in you during the self-contemplations and exercises, it would be useful to have a pencil and paper at hand, in order to write these down using key words.

So that you may totally concentrate on any movement or process you may go through in your inner being, you should close your eyes at the appropriate places and give yourself time to observe the rising pictures and thoughts that form in you.

While the answer to the question that you direct toward yourself takes on the form of pictures, it would be good to listen to quiet music as accompaniment to the phases of inward contemplation, of self-observation. A CD with appropriate music is included with this booklet.

Are You Who You Think You Are?

Every person has a name that, to the authorities and civil servants, identifies who he is from birth on. This is not meant to be put into question here. The following explanations and exercises want much more to give the individual the possibility to make himself aware of who he is in the multiplicity of his human person, of his personality. And then, based on his self-recognition, he can actively begin to shape his own inner and outer life, and set out toward the place where his soul once came from—toward the eternal homeland, the pure Being, toward God, our heavenly Father.

For many people, their first and last names, their title and occupational description are of great significance, for their name together with its attributes identifies who they are. The name represents the person, so to speak, what and how he presents himself and what of him is visible externally to his environment and to his fellow men.

If a name is mentioned, then in those fellow men who know the person, a certain picture emerges immediately—a picture of the specific personality of the person with all its facets. This is how the others see him, because this is how he presents and shows himself. This is how "one knows him." His "good name" vouches, so to speak, for his prestige, character and trustworthiness.

An example: Two friends meet. One mentions the name of "Anne" and talks about a "Mr. Hubert, General Director."* His conversation partner nods and says, "I know her" and "I know him." He may even say, "I know her well" or "I know him well," and mean this sincerely.

Let us stop at this point and ask: Does he really know Anne? He has a certain picture of her and signals to his friend that it is the person of whom the other just spoke. But does he really know her?

And what about Mr. Hubert, General Director? Do both friends really know him? *What* do they know about him? For example, they know his external appearance, some of his ways of behaving, perhaps his office and his car. If they know him "well," then perhaps this word formulation refers to something more, to his way of speaking, to some of his smaller human characteristics, to his favorite foods, the brand of his cigarettes and other things. The term for all of this is then the name Mr. Hubert, General Director.

----

* The name is invented. I do not know anyone by this name.

But based on all of this, can we already say that we know him? Is he really who he shows himself to be?

Dear reader, dear brothers and sisters, this is not all about a certain person whose name I thought up as an example. Instead, it refers to wanting to get to the bottom of some human habits and statements together, that is, to question them, and at that, not by looking at others but by looking at ourselves in the first place. We want to ask the question: Are we, every single one of us, *the* person whom we pass ourselves off as and whom we briefly describe with our name, and if the situation warrants it, with our title, perhaps complemented with an indication of our profession, which identifies our position in society? Do we know who hides behind the façade, who bears our name and everything that goes with it, yes, who perhaps day by day more or less successfully hides behind these?

The fewest people know themselves. They just go through their days, satisfied with their name and their appearance which they have built up and shaped through their way of speaking and acting, through their success in their profession and in society or by acquiring other honors and dignities, money and possessions or some position or other.

But of what takes place behind, or under, their external expressions, they are hardly aware themselves.

To remain with our example, perhaps Mr. Huber, General Director, does not know himself what he really thinks and feels, when he, for example, fires an employee with deeply regretful words, or when he consistently waits on the firm's boss with many friendly gestures and compliments. Based on his large and regular donations, he may think himself a generous person, or even a benefactor of mankind, because he seldom takes an account of his real motives and reasons. He lives in the belief that he is who he seems to be.

Many thus identify themselves with the picture they have of themselves, which in many facets is a sham, that is, a self-deception. The one who shies away from the effort of looking behind his own mask, his comportment, also does not get to know himself. Through this superficial pattern of behavior, a person wastes his life on Earth. He passes up the chances to improve the true quality of his life, his character, because a person who does not know himself, cannot change himself either.

Whoever closely observes the condition of today's world, will doubtless agree: Most people apparently do not know who they are. They give their title, their first and last names, their area of competence and office; they speak strong words, perhaps show themselves as jovial and caring, and no one knows whether they really are what they show themselves to be—or whether their title and names haven't become a hidden "wanted poster" in the course of their life on Earth, for title, first and last names and other nice-sounding by-lines can cover up a lot, for example, envy, hatred, unscrupulousness, clever exploitation of others, corruption and much more.

As on a small scale, so on a large one: Anyone who thinks he's the ultimate is of the opinion that he deserves the largest piece of the cake—the other guy, his fellow man, "the guy down there," has to be satisfied with the crumbs. Such a person seldom questions himself, perhaps not even when the harvest follows his sowing and the truth comes to light. Then, mostly—in the small things of our daily life, as in the large—the "other guy's to blame." Self-justification, the rigid image of himself, of his conviction about his the self-worth associated with his name and appearance, allows no other reaction.

The face that we show to the outside world and that is identified with our name is often not our true face. Do we ourselves know who we really are?

The following thought-up example of a person is called "Anne," she could just as easily be called by any other name.

Anne is generally considered to be a friendly, well-meaning contemporary, and she herself thinks so, too. She enjoys the trust of her large circle of acquaintances and people often ask her for advice. She is sociable, helpful and communicative. Anne herself would recognize this description and say, "Yes, that's me."

And so, this brief outline of an image is called Anne. But is this really her? She could get to know herself better if she were to not only take a look at what she says and does, but also at what lies behind what she does, at her motivations, her secret intentions, her hidden reasons for what she does. Perhaps behind her seeming friendly face, totally different types of thoughts and feelings about her fellow man tumble about, for "Anne" could be, for example, constantly on the lookout to register the faults and weaknesses of others and collect information to cleverly use to her own advantage when the occasion arises.

If Anne were to ask herself why she offers her help here or there, she could discover that behind this, for example, there is a desire to look good in front of her neighbor, perhaps as clever, selfless, trustworthy and a faithful friend. If she were to then ask why she wants to give others this picture of herself, she may figure out that she feels the urge to stand above her fellow man, to see herself as a better, cleverer, more important, etc., person. If she has come thus far in self-recognition, she can also still ask herself why she needs this arrogance, what weaknesses she wants to cover up or compensate for it.

But our fellow man, whom we call "Anne" in our example, does *not* ask "why"—as most people do not. She is satisfied with "I'm Anne" or "My name is Anne." She herself does not know what may be hidden behind the positive façade "Anne." And all those who likewise have not come to recognize their own underhandedness, repenting of it and clearing it up, also think just like Anne.

But the one who investigates his own hidden motives and clears up these negative aspects with the Spirit of the Christ of God, thus expanding his consciousness, can perceive things more deeply as a result. For him, his fellow man is an open book. He recognizes him, because he has come to know himself.

Dear reader, dear brothers, dear sisters, life on Earth could be very interesting for many a person if he were to question his thoughts, words and actions, if he were to ask whether his words, for example, are in accord with his thoughts, or his actions with his thoughts, words and feelings.

Anyone who wants to investigate himself, in order to find out who actually romps about behind his name, has to first ask at the moment what or who lies hidden behind his feelings, thoughts, words and actions. Another step would then be to analyze what he has realized, in order to find the root of the possible evil by asking the question of *why* he is divided and what lies behind this dividedness, what his purpose is with it. For it is the reason for a person's behavior patterns that is what the person actually is, and not what he pretends to be.

In many cases the name of a person is not in accord with what is associated with it. Self-analysis can bring to light a totally different person, who, for example, no longer corresponds to his title, his names, his position, his occupation. And so, the one who does not examine himself will also not recognize what he really is.

Many a one could now protest and say, "Well, it may very well be that my life—as with most people—shows a certain ambiguity. But why should

I take the effort to recognize myself? Why should I know more about myself than I already do? I feel good where I'm at, and am quite content with my life. So, as far as I'm concerned, things can keep going the way they are till the end of my life."

Many think this way because they do not know what the meaning and purpose of their life on Earth is all about. But on the one hand, the situation in one's life can change from one day to the next in anyone's life, when, according to the law of sowing and reaping, those things come toward him which he sowed and were not so good, and which he did not clear up. On the other hand, our life does not come to an end with the death of our body. Our life continues in the beyond—though without the masks behind which we hid, here on Earth, our true face, our not so good character traits.

We, that is, the soul, leave the material shell of our coarse-material body behind on the Earth, including all that which was so important to us as a human being, for example, our title, our name, all our possessions. But our *true* character traits, which are the result of the *contents* of our feelings, sensations, thoughts, words and deeds, our real identity which we kept hidden as a human being, that is, our burdens, we take with us. They form the engraving of our soul. This alone, then determines our life in the beyond.

There, we can no longer hide anything; everything is manifest. As a soul, we then must suffer painfully what we did to others with our underhandedness, everything that we caused to our fellow man. The excuse, "the other one is to blame" is then no longer of use to us. We alone are responsible for what we emit in the five components, this means, in our feelings, sensations, thoughts, words and actions. And what we have emitted, which is also what we have sown, is what we will in turn reap.

Our seed, our contrary behavior, is engraved in our soul as well as stored in the repository stars of the purification planes. With certain planetary constellations, our inputs then radiate back into us. If we then are on Earth as a human being, what hits us now is only what we have caused ourselves. The effects then show themselves in the form of need, worry, suffering and sorrow, illness and other blows of fate. And so, we ourselves forge our own fate.

Nonetheless, during our days on Earth we receive promptings over and over again from the energy of the day, pointers which give us the opportunity to recognize that burdens in our soul—that is, the sinfulness, the inputs we have stored—are in the process of becoming active. If we do not pay attention to these warnings, that is, if we fail to recognize ourselves in good time, then over the short or long term we will feel the effects, when the repository stars radiate back to us on Earth the negative energies we once emitted.

This is why it is so important to use every opportunity to gain in self-recognition, in order to become aware of who we really are behind our masks.

Now and again we are shocked by our evil thoughts and desires. Instead of analyzing them, we repress the message from our subconscious and practice our veiling tactics. These develop into a cover-up behavior pattern, and this, in turn, into falsity and lies. A person caught up in this spinning orbit acts differently than he really is.

A person who wants to recognize himself, that is, who wants to find his way to his subconscious and to the inputs he has stored, to the engravings in his soul—no matter from which incarnation these came—has to question himself from without to within. As with an onion, we have to peel back layer by layer, in order to find out what all is present in our subconscious and in the soul, hidden there, so to speak.

With the help of the Spirit of God, who dwells in each one of us, much is possible for each person, for the almighty, eternal spirit of love does not want us to journey over and over again from this side of life as soul into the beyond and then from the beyond into this side of life again. God, our eternal Father, also doesn't want us to experience over and over again the harvest of our seed, in need, ignominy, misfortune and suffering. He does not want that we, blind and unfree, waste the life energy given to us by keeping up our façade, securing and polishing our masks. God, the eternal giver of all that is good, wants so much to take our burdens from us, if we surrender them to Him in good time, based on our self-recognition and our clearing them up. He wants us to walk the light-filled road joyfully and with light steps, the road which leads us home into the eternal kingdom, there where He and our brothers and sisters in heaven are waiting for us.

The Earth is nothing more than a school for all people, whether beggar or king, prince or princess, duke or duchess, whether doctor, professor, excellency, eminence, honorable and the like.

No matter a person's social position in name or possessions, anyone who does not question himself does not know himself. And the one who does not examine himself has wasted his life on Earth. But the one who sees his life on Earth as a school where he can learn about himself, will soon be confronted with his ego, with his egotism that has many facets. These are a part of his actual identity, a part of the engravings on his soul, which it takes with itself into the beyond after the death of its body and with which it may eventually return as a human being to this side of life.

A person finds the different layers of his inputs only when he strives day after day to look *behind* his façade, *behind* his old habits, which have become behavior patterns in him, and to analyze what is stored there. This is done, for example, when we always ask ourselves the question "why?": Why do I act this way? Why do I feel pushed by this or that? Why was I silent about that in our conversation? Why am I embarrassed when I meet this or that person? Why do I help this person and not that one? … and many other similar things.

We should pay no further attention to the behavior of *others* toward us. We recognize *our* part in what occurred and question this. First of all, we should figure out how we acted toward our fellow man, what we did to him and how he may have suffered because of it. In this, we should not forget the factor of life force by asking: How often have we taken life energy from our neighbor by forcing him subtly, as a wily tactician with seeming logical arguments, to do something that was to our advantage and brought us even more gain?

When a person reaches this realization, remorse and a vow to improve have to come up in him, because without a remorse of the conscience there is no way to clear up and make amends. The result of such an inner movement would be that the remorseful person no longer does the same or similar thing. It is only then that the engraving in the soul is erased. It is only in this way that we show our true colors and, from our hypocrisy, reach truthfulness via recognition.

And so, we must clear the jungle of our human ego in order to figure out what threads and ropes, lianas, so to speak, we have tied together and on which we have swung and swing through our life, and which liana pathways we have set up to bind others to us.

We have an immortal soul. Inasmuch as it is not burdened, that is, as a spirit being, it is purity, love, beauty, eternal youth—a being in the image of God. If our goal is to strive toward this again, just as Jesus called on us to ... *be perfect as your heavenly Father is perfect ...,* then, among other things, the light of recognition could shine for many a one, and his pathways would become more light-filled.

Dear reader, dear brothers and sisters, whether we want to accept it or not, every person is in the school of life, Earth, to recognize himself and to perfect himself, for our soul shall return to the eternal Father-house. This is why as human beings we have to learn to apply the cosmic laws, which are the love, freedom and unity. From a spiritual point of view, everyone, the one more, the other less, needs to go through a metamorphosis; like a butterfly, he should emerge from the chrysalis of human personalness which is egocentric, from the all-too-human, the base, toward the divine I Am, which is impersonal.

And even if we journey through ever so many lives on Earth—each one of us is on his way to his divine origin. Even if we go through many pupations, spinning ourselves in and emerging again, from soul to human being and from human being to soul—at some point in time we will have emerged from our cocoon for the last time. Our spiritual metamorphosis is then finished. Like the caterpillar which becomes a butterfly, we raise our wings into the air toward the spiritual sun and return to our origin which is divine. Then we have become again the image of our eternal Father.

A being in God is impersonal, and this means that like all pure beings, it lives in the stream of infinity and is, like all divine beings, the personified spiritual law, God, in its multifarious mentality.

Every divine being, called spirit being, is thus the law of unity of the All and not the personal law, which each person has created for himself in the causal law of the Fall through the five previously mentioned components. Every spirit being has its specific name, which vibrates in the great all-harmony of unity.

We human beings do not know our heavenly name. But we do know where our path should go. We should turn back into the eternal Father-house, into the Kingdom of God, into the eternal law of love.

This is why we should use our day, yes, every minute, every moment of our day, to get to know ourselves ever more deeply and encompassingly, so that we can take the further steps that lead us home.

There are many different possibilities for getting to know oneself. Every learning opportunity begins, however, with self-examination and self-observation, and from this, can come self-recognition. A help in this would be, for example, to draw on a matrix an impersonal, nameless human image of faultless character, of good, God-pleasing characteristics. This human image could become a guiding image of self-recognition for many a person.

I call such a guiding image the "nameless matrix-person," the impersonal Being, which is the life in God.

The nameless matrix-person points out how the human image should be in order to become the image of God: a faultless person of character who lives in full awareness. The ideal picture of the nameless matrix-person already bears traits of the divine being, which we are in our innermost being, and to which we shall become again in order to return home, to our homeland in the light.

This image however, also points out who the individual really is as a human being when he compares his recognition-picture and his name, which are often used as a signboard, a façade, with the nameless matrix-person.

First of all, we now want to portray our personal recognition-picture; secondly, we will draw the ideal picture of perfect life, the matrix-person. Please keep paper and pencil at hand in order to perhaps take some notes later.

First, we want to more or less observe ourselves from without, to observe the person who bears our name, our estimation of ourselves. So at this point, we do not want to plumb any depths, but instead take a simple and plain look at the roles we play out daily.

We want to ask ourselves the question: Who am I? Or: Who do I think I am?

Because our sense of sight influences all other senses the strongest, including our feelings and thoughts, we close our eyes to better concentrate on ourselves while we let these questions resound in us. If we also take up an upright posture, we gain somewhat more distance from our whirling of our thoughts, which could distract us from an honest observation of our self-images.

And so, we sit upright and place both feet on the floor. The backs of our hands rest on our lap and we draw them close to our body. We keep our head up straight.

Now we breathe deeply a few times in and out. While doing this, we concentrate on our breathing, how it comes and goes.

Through this relaxed posture and through the concentration on our breathing, we become calmer. Our thoughts recede—including those which already want to curiously figure out what may lie in us. Very gradually they become totally insignificant. This is important, because every wishful thought can affect our recognition-picture and change it, that is, falsify it. As a first step, we want to observe ourselves just as we would normally see and feel ourselves.

> We breathe deeply in and out,
> in and out,
> in and out,
> in and out,
> in and out.
> Our breathing is now calm and deep.
> Calm and deep is our breathing.
> Now, we let it breathe.

In our thoughts, we now ask ourselves the question:

"Who am I?" so that we can bring before our eyes, that is, bring to our awareness, who we are, from our perspective. The one who wants to, can speak this question out loud, but he should direct it to himself.

Dear reader, dear brother, dear sister, now your image forms in your consciousness. It is you and your name, and includes your title, occupation, position or any other identifying factors belonging to you.

Observe your image. It is your habitual, every-day image.

As a second step, we will now go deeper. In your thoughts and awareness, let what you just got in association with yourself, including your first and last names, your title and occupation, vibrate and resound *into your inner being*. In this way you will establish communication with your personal, energetic image, where many a thing is played out in your everyday life without your being aware of it .

Let your image unfold itself in your inner space. Your inner, under-the-surface "for and against" will become more and more active. This vibrating complex-person very gradually fans out, for by observing your image and its reflection in your subconscious, you stimulate analytical thought processes in your consciousness which break down the "for and against" and lead you to self-recognition—if you want.

This self-observation is an energetic communication. Allow this to happen! What develops from this are images that you can see, with sequential pictures of many different situations and occasions which lead your past and present before your eyes. In this sequence of pictures you recognize what you want and do not want to accept about yourself during your daily life and awareness, and therefore push to the side and ignore. You now grasp what hides behind your feelings, sensations, thoughts, words and actions. You also experience the world of your repressed desires and passions.

Whatever it may be that is given for you to recognize, let it happen! It offers you the chance to learn more about yourself. You can use this, if you want.

What you now experience about yourself is a part of your true character. Take the time to observe yourself, but also to listen to yourself in all the "for and against," questioning whether this character trait fits with the façade-image that bears your name.

If you should now discover not-so-nice things in and on you—do not recoil in shock. Do not again press it back into your subconscious. It is only what we become aware of that we can also change. Self-recognition is a gift of grace.

And so, let the movement in your subconscious come up; let the turmoil, the images, come alive in your consciousness.

While this takes place, if you would like to, close your eyes and listen to soft music.

If you would like to, open your eyes in order to perhaps write down some of what moved you.

As a further exercise, we now focus exclusively on our first name. Think the following three words: "I am," for example, "Anne." Or: "I am Fred." Think or speak your first name into yourself.

In these three words, "I am," for example, "Anne," you are addressing yourself. With your first name, without the addition of title or last name, you again establish communication with other aspects of your nature. The result is another different recognition-picture than what you would get with your full name.

Again you experience pictures in your consciousness, pictorial portraits that on the one hand, come from your soul, and on the other, from your subconscious. And so, they are reflections from the soul sphere and from the subconscious.

In this sequence of pictures, you again experience yourself. You experience situations and occurrences, your feelings, your desires and thoughts. Much of what you have pushed to the side and repressed till now will become active in your consciousness, that is, you will become aware of them. If you really want to shed light on and throughout yourself, then take time for this self-observation.

Again you can close your eyes and listen to soft music. You determine for yourself when you open your eyes to take short notes.

As a next step, if you want to, let your first and last names, your titles, and if you consider it important, your profession or occupation come to life in your consciousness.

This means to say now, "My name is Mr.," "… Mrs.," "… Dr.," "Professor," then the first and last names, and perhaps even the occupation.

Remain concentrated in your thoughts on all the attributes that are a part of this expanded name identity.

With your statement "My name is …," you have addressed yourself and raised corresponding pictorial portraits from your subconscious, which will be decoded in your consciousness if you want. These images again show you your true face, what you actually felt, thought, spoke and why you acted as you did. Among other things, they are occurrences and situations which you may have kept hidden from your surroundings, perhaps from the public eye. It can also be an exposure of intentions and self-serving goals that we covered over with seemingly positive words and actions. Such secretive games with others are deceptions, with which we put on a mask, as it were. If these maskings gradually become engravings, which hide our egoism in a laughing and seemingly kind way, then we often no longer know ourselves, who we really are.

Let us make ourselves aware of the fact that the subconscious cannot think; it does not deceive—it brings out what we really are.

What's left for you to do now is to take the contents of these picture sequences, which actually point out your behavior patterns, and compare them with what you, for example, pretend to be.

Take time to observe yourself in your pictures and to hear what you have placed as contents in your behavior.

What your subconscious releases, what rises and shows itself in pictures, is a part of your life-film, of your past. They are your inputs in the stars of fate, the repository stars, and that is what you are.

If you want let your inner self-contemplation be accompanied by the soft sounds of music.

Now close your eyes. Think, or say: "My name is…," with titles, first and last names, perhaps also occupation.

If you would like to, write down what moved you a great deal.

We now practice the same thing again.

Once again, close your eyes and address yourself with your title, with your first and last names and perhaps with your occupation.

By addressing yourself this way you may establish contact via your subconscious with a further planetary constellation which determines your day today. What then develops in your consciousness are the corresponding pictures that may point out totally different aspects of your inputs than the previous picture sequences. But what you become aware of is just as much a part of you as what you were already able to recognize.

And so, say to yourself: "My name is …" using your full name and everything that goes with it.

Feel into these pictures and let them come alive in you. Experience what takes place behind your patterns of behavior, yourself. It can be that in the picture sequences your words are very caring and your actions seem selfless. But register very exactly whether what you say and do correspond to what you think. It could be that you think other than you speak and act. For example, behind your kind, selfless actions, could hide the thought that you want to receive something appropriate for this, even if it be praise and recognition, or that you want to gain people for a certain purpose or it could be other things.

It is not the caring words or the seemingly pure actions that are taken in by your subconscious, by your soul particles and the repository stars, but much more that which lies *behind* your way of behaving. This is what you really are.

Dear brothers, dear sisters, let us take courage to confront our less nice character traits that we have kept hidden behind our masks, behind our façade! Only the un-good, which, *unrecognized*, tosses and turns, stewing and smoldering under the surface, is what weighs down and darkens our mood. It does not let us become joyful, and makes us anxious, restless, narrow-minded and unfree.

Self-recognition is truly the first step to improvement, because what we have once clearly grasped can also be dissolved with the help of the Redeemer and Liberator in us, Christ. He knows us through and through, anyway. His help is certain because He always wants the best for us.

Dear brother, dear sister, and so, observe yourself in the sequence of pictures. And remember that we are responsible for our feeling, sensing, thinking, speaking and acting, ourselves. We cannot push the blame onto our neighbor. Only his part will come to him, and that has to do only with him and God.

So if you would like to, take notes on the important points. Give yourself time for this, and listen to soft music while doing so.

Based on the self-recognition you have attained, it is now possible for you to give yourself the answer, as to whether your title, your first and last names, your occupation and other aspects of your "self-images," your everyday face, so to speak, fit with your *true* face and thus with the inputs you have placed into your subconscious, into your soul and into the corresponding repository planets.

So, are you at one with your self—or is divisiveness to be noted?

You now can see it yourself. Through these exercises, the veils that you had laid over your subconscious have been aired a bit. The not-so-good which came to the fore will not please many a one. But it will be of no use to us to quickly draw the veils closed, to put the masks on again and to remain the same under the surface. For every single one of us, the day will come when every mask will fall. And no matter what it happens to be—we do not have to remain this way!

Many people nevertheless tend to want to avoid the uncomfortable. Instead of turning within, with the aim to change his character for the good, the one or the other simply changes his mask to keep up his disguise. And the one who has recognized and cleared up little in himself is easily deceived by this.

In this way a person who places himself above his fellow man can one day come to the point where, wearing a hair shirt, so to speak, he behaves remorsefully or even subserviently. But through this alone, nothing has yet changed in his character, in his arrogance. Behind the new mask he will probably continue to belittle and deride his neighbor—until he recognizes his wrong attitude, clears it up with the help and strength of the Christ of God and henceforth shows toward his fellow brothers and sisters more and more respect, good will and appreciation.

One can see a lot of mask-changing in this world.

So that we can compare the inputs we have recognized with our origin, the true Being, I would like to set up a nameless matrix-person with you in thought. On this matrix one can see a person who reflects the laws of the universe, whose subconscious carries only the *memories* of a past that has been overcome and the life-programs that every person needs for his life on Earth. When the time has come to emerge from the cocoon, the purified and cleansed soul will soar into the air like a butterfly, beyond space and time, beyond the purification planes, to go into the Kingdom of God as a divine being.

And so, we set up such a person on a matrix that we have thought out. I call it the nameless matrix-person, because it is no longer tied to the earthly-human, the all-too-human, to all the programs of wanting to be and to have which represent our human name.

We remain in the previously described sitting posture. If you would like to, close your eyes during this inward journey, so that you may better concentrate.

Allow no thoughts in. Try to concentrate on the matrix image that lies before you.

Perhaps you have become somewhat restless through the exercises and explanations. For this reason, watch your breathing once again.

Breathe consciously. The more consciously you breathe, the calmer you become and the better you can concentrate, because your tumultuous thoughts recede from you.

Accompany your inhaling and exhaling with your sensations. Listen to your breathing, how it comes and goes.

You breathe consciously, in and out,
in and out.
The thoughts that move you recede.
They become more and more calm.
You are breathing consciously.

Your conscious breathing is supported by soft, relaxing music.

Now, you let it breathe.

Allow no thoughts in. Your breathing is calm and deep. You are calm and relaxed.

If you would like to, draw with the paintbrush of your thoughts, with your power of imagination and your senses, a matrix upon which can be seen the outline of a person. Your matrix-person is, like you, male or female.

It is helpful to close your eyes, over and over again, while the matrix-person takes on shape in your consciousness more and more , as in the following explanation.

The matrix-person, which can become for you a guiding image to perfection, develops starting with the head. On our matrix we now sketch—this means that each one uses the paintbrush of his own imagination and senses—a beautifully formed human face with a high forehead, shining eyes and nobly formed brows. Fitting with a finely cut facial form, we draw a nose and ears that are in balance. The cheekbones are only lightly indicated. We draw in an even mouth; the lips are very nice and unobtrusive. We lead the chin harmoniously into the neck, which carries the head. We frame the head with a modest but nice hairdo.

We continue to develop the matrix-person. Straight shoulders emerge; with a male principle they are strong and able, with the female, gentler and soft. With the male matrix-person, we draw strong, well-formed arms and strong hands using the paintbrush of our imagination and of our senses, and with the female principle, we draw in slender, well-formed arms and fine-fingered hands. With the male as well as female matrix-person, we draw well-formed fingernails.

We draw in the male body as athletic, but slender. The female matrix-person is slender, but not too thin.

Every picture corresponds to a male, or female, ideal picture. With the male type, we draw in strong legs, with the female principle, on the other hand, slender, well formed, with nice ankles. With the male as well as female matrix-persons, we draw in feet that correspond to the harmonious and balanced body.

The development of the matrix-person, which can be a guiding image for us, was and is under the motto: "I am only a guest on the Earth." In this spirit—"I am only a guest on the Earth"—its subconscious is also programmed. This memory bank contains memories of past days, perhaps from childhood, from the parental home, from the parents, grandparents, the relatives, from youth, the school, studies, choice of occupation, the training for a profession and its practice, and so on. In the consciousness is also found these picture-engravings, the roadmap of its present life, further stores of information like daily work and the nice and less nice occurrences that are a part of it, the plans for the day, the acquaintances, friendships, family events and experiences and much more. The consciousness of the matrix-person is as tranquil as a calm lake.

For the matrix-person, the past is gone but not forgotten. He is aware that the roadmap of his life on Earth consists of all the situations, events and learning steps he takes. He is also aware that he has brought a part of them from his previous incarnations into this life on Earth. In the consciousness and subconscious of the matrix-person is nothing suspicious, nothing hurtful. The contents of his five components, that is, of his feeling, sensing, thinking, speaking and acting are uprightness, honesty, devotion of self, a willingness to sacrifice and self-sacrifice as well. His character traits radiate understanding and tolerance. The subconscious is the same as the consciousness. In both memory banks there is nothing compelling or binding, nothing expecting or demanding, that is, there is nothing that is not good.

The whole body of the matrix-person radiates calm, sovereignty, clarity, freshness, purity, freedom, openness, balance in all things as well as helpfulness, kindness and inner steadfastness. It radiates the equilibrium of life. Through a free and peaceful consciousness and subconscious, what radiates out is a closeness to all people and beings, the unity with the nature realms, with the cosmos.

The impersonal, cosmic, all-ruling law, the I AM, streams through the body of the matrix-person and charges every cell with higher vitality. Every organ, all the muscles and muscle fibers, bones, blood and lymph vessels, all nerves and nerve systems, glands and hormones, all the components of the body are in harmony with one another and vibrate in harmonious accord with the cosmic All-harmony.

The matrix-person, our guiding image, radiates health and happiness. The whole person is a balanced, radiating image.

A pure, elegantly proportioned, youthful, agile, supple and balanced body radiates from the matrix. It conveys security, confidence, dependability and beauty to us.

And so, the nameless matrix-person is now standing before your spiritual eyes, irradiated by the cosmic, eternal I AM. It has no name, no façade, nothing hidden. It is simply the one who it is, through and through. It is at one with itself and at one with the life. It *is*.

Observe this image. Let its radiation take effect on you. Perhaps it will awaken in your inner being the longing for what the matrix-person is.

While you observe this image and let it take effect in your inner being, listen to quiet music.

Anyone who has acquired a small insight into his five components, into his smaller or greater underhandedness, sees the difference between himself and the person on the matrix.

Deep in our soul, in the very basis of our soul, is our true being, our pure spirit body, which is far more beautiful than the person on the matrix.

Each one of us determines his life on Earth himself. Each one of us decides daily about our own personal process of development and becoming. Either we develop our true being and find our way into the very basis of our soul, or we shadow our soul and subconscious through our egotism and become the personified wanting to be and to have which says: "Me, me—everything only for me."

Dear brother, dear sister, the nameless matrix-person could show you the steps which lead you to your true being, but, of course, only when you let it become your example, when you draw a comparison between yourself and the nameless matrix-person and with the help of the spirit of infinity repent of your human traits, clear them up and no longer do them.

Only in this way can the guiding image to perfection come alive in you and radiate to you again and again what you should put into practice in your daily life in order to grow closer to the matrix-person. The salvation comes from within, from the source of life, God. The guiding image could be helpful to you to approach your true origin.

If you would like to, here are some more exercises for you to do.

Pictorially, take the nameless matrix-person and place it over your body, or put this image on, as if you were putting on your clothes. During the following inner process, close your eyes briefly again and again. Remain calm and relaxed.

Now, become aware of your name. Your first and last names, perhaps your occupation and title, which you now express in your thoughts, radiate into the nameless matrix-person. If you feel the discrepancy between yourself and the matrix-person, then ask yourself, whether your values, which you may connect with your name, fit with the nameless matrix-person, and whether you are what you behave like with your affected behavior, with your disguise, as it were.

If you do not avoid the conflict between yourself and the image, then it radiates the answer to you, for example, what you should be and are not. This would be the moment of self-recognition; this would be the moment of decision.

Either you avoid the conflict, or you let the answer simply stand—or you take a step toward your example, by analyzing what you have recognized in order to find the root, the cause, which you then repent of in your thoughts, resolving for the positive which your guiding image radiates to you.

If you want to have a conversation with a person based on the recognitions you have newly acquired, in order to ask for forgiveness, then do it after this radiation of recognition.

So that you have time to observe yourself, to perhaps analyze your inner conflicts which are the gateway to self-recognition, and to enter your good resolutions into your consciousness, and perhaps note these briefly down, listen to quiet music.

The more you work with the nameless matrix-person, the more it becomes real. This means that your conscience becomes more active, so that in situations and with egocentric statements, the question automatically comes up, whether you are acting the way your guiding image, the matrix-person, demonstrates to you.

As soon as you have taken in such and similar impulses, something comes into movement in your subconscious, because your behavior is not in accordance with your guiding image.

By working through the conflict that emerges in you because of this, you experience pictures in your consciousness. These could be symbols that should then be analyzed by you. But they could also be sequences of pictures in which you can recognize very exactly your "for" and "against."

Through an honest, that is, merciless, analysis, you will very gradually get to the basis of your so-being, of how you are at the moment.

If you have questioned yourself, that is, analyzed your way of behaving and your pretentious comportment, then compare your evaluation with the matrix-person, which has become your conscience, and ask yourself whether you are prepared to feel remorse for the all-too-human aspects, that is, for your negativity, and to clear it up.

If you are prepared to do this, then ask the spirit of infinity, God in you, or the Christ of God, your Redeemer, for support and help. If your request is sincere and honest, then you can be sure that you will be helped to grow closer to your example, your guiding image to perfection.

In your consciousness, hold firmly onto the aspects which you perceive are a step toward the perfection of your true nature, and strive to fulfill these principles of the laws of inner life.

In case you want to take a few short notes, you may do so. In the meantime, do listen to a little quiet music.

Our physical body is, as mentioned, the product of the contents of our five components of feeling, sensing, thinking, speaking and acting. We also describe our body as a body of feelings and thoughts. We ourselves marked and shaped our body according to what we placed into the five components. And so, our body is a manifestation and a self-manipulation, so to speak, through the contents of our five components.

Let us become aware that all the functions of our body are in communication with our brain and speak to us.

Dear brother, dear sister, the more often you observe the nameless matrix-person and let it work on you, the more you can feel how signals of strength, of harmony, of peace, security, confidence, secureness and much more emanate from it. Remember, the matrix-person radiates; your body reacts and gives signals. The reactions and signals of your body are the language of your cells and organs.

If you would like to take some more notes, then do so. Remain in inner calm and in closeness to your guiding image. While doing so, listen to soft music again.

The person who conscientiously works with his guiding image, the nameless matrix-person, very gradually gains insight into the world of his thoughts, into the restlessness, the anxiety, the hectic pace, the animosity, spitefulness, the un-reliability and incompatibility which always dis-gruntle us and make us disharmonious. The guiding image to perfection wants to help each one of us find the contents of these discrepancies.

Become a tracker of the contents of your be-havior patterns, in order to figure out what opposes your guiding image to perfection! But ask yourself as well whether your behavior—everything that you bring out into the light of day through the analysis of your thinking and acting—corresponds to your title, to your name and occupation, that is, whether you are *this* or *that* which you pretend to be with your name. With one single recognition, masks are not gotten rid of once and for all. There are always new aspects or parts of these to be discovered.

If you would like to, move your body, stretch your arms and legs. Feel into your soul and into your body.

Are you your name? Is your name, or are you, what you pass yourself off as or as you identify yourself? Or are you a totally different person behind your façade?

Only you can answer this. You are the one who made the comparison between yourself and the nameless matrix-person.

Let us again make ourselves aware of the fact that when we no longer bear our physical shell, because our soul is in the beyond, then nothing, but nothing that today has all-too-human value to us is significant. In our soul we take with us only what we have placed *into* the five components of feeling, sensing, thinking, speaking and acting; it is what lies *behind* our behavior patterns. Each one of the five components will be measured and weighed by the cosmic scales, by the stars, and then assigned to the corresponding planetary con-stellation.

Based on the principle of sending and receiving, we are constantly under the control of countless planets which act and react according to the causal law. This is the indescribable bookkeeping of the universe. It is absolutely just.

What we must constantly remember is that the contents of the behavior of others does not enter our soul. What our neighbor thinks and says has nothing to do with us. If his behavior upsets us, we can recognize in this that we have the same or similar thing in us. Only what goes out from us, our feeling, sensing, thinking, speaking and acting, is what comes back into us again—unless we make the world of thoughts of someone else our own, that is, when we are imitators or let others influence us, determining things for us, indoctrinating and manipulating us. The effects that result from this are then related to the one as well as to the other, to the one who controlled things and the one who let himself be controlled. The result of this can be a common causality. Then both sit in the same boat and perhaps are rowing toward a new bank to-gether—a new incarnation. For example, both go into a new incarnation, in order to meet at some point and clear up whatever has bound the two to each other. Because of this, on the Earth there is no encounter without a reason, without a cause.

Each day gives us the opportunity for self-recognition. A person who uses the day for this, to find his self, his all-too-human aspects, and to get rid of these, acts in a wise way, because none of us know when our last hour on Earth will strike. After our physical death, we will either go into the beyond as a light-filled soul and aware of our true Self, or we go into the beyond as a soul surrounded by overestimation, blind and imprisoned by the world. As the latter, and in our fine-material body, we will at first continue to behave as if we were his excellency, his eminence, a prince, duke, duchess, princess, manager, Mr. or Mrs., Dr., Professor, and so on.

However, nothing, but really nothing that is world-oriented has value in the beyond. As a soul we are of the opinion that we are still the same as what we pretended to be as human beings. This continues until a planetary constellation irradiates us with the corresponding inputs that are active in it. And then, many a soul is indignant to learn that it should be what it now experiences in and on itself, and that it deserves the surroundings in which it now finds itself.

Just as ignorant about its true character state as it was as a human being, the soul feels that it has been unjustly treated. But all complaining and moaning is of no use—the causal computer, the law of cause and effect, does not deceive itself.

As a soul we are in expiation which goes with the pain we caused others at some point in time.

We suffer under what we have sown, until we become aware of the Christ of God, who is our Redeemer and Savior, and we follow the path of remorse, asking for forgiveness and forgiving.

God's all-ruling hand is selfless and thus, impersonal. God does not look at our external pretentious behavior. He sees us just as He has created us: pure, with the absolute values of the I AM, the law of infinity. Through Moses, God gave us the Ten Commandments and Jesus, the Christ, gave us the Sermon on the Mount. And so, we have extensive instructions to work with, so that daily, in every situation, we can question and examine whether the contents of our thinking, speaking and acting correspond to the Commandments of God and the Sermon on the Mount of Jesus.

Remember: God, our Father in Christ, our Redeemer, wants the best for us. Untiringly, the mighty spirit of harmony and of peace, the might of the great, all-encompassing love, knocks at the gate to our heart. God, the unending love, leaves us the freedom to either open, but also to close, or keep closed, this gateway.

Every day you have many opportunities to hear the knocking of the Spirit of God, for instance, via your conscience—or when you get upset about someone, or when you use your name and the aura associated with it, the prestige, as a means to an end, and much more.

Worthy reader, dear brother, dear sister, the nameless matrix-person, a guiding image to self-recognition, can accompany you through each day and become a good, faithful friend—if you let this image come alive, by not only resolving to question yourself, but by doing it every day in the many situations, and by comparing your behavior again and again with the nameless matrix-person, your guiding image.

With all my heart, I wish that you, in connection with your guiding image, the nameless matrix-person, may recognize your all-too-human aspects and with the help of the Christ of God, our Redeemer, that you repent of them and clear them up. And when you no longer do what you have recognized, the gateway to inner life will open for you more and more, and in your heart you will recognize the divinity, which God, the Father of us all, breathed into you. In this way, you can increasingly go through an ever more fulfilled life, more free, active, joyful and confident.

Dear brother, dear sister, many brothers and sisters are struggling for the inner light. The fight with our shadows is given to each one of us, to get rid of them so that it become ever more light-filled in us.

Christ, our Redeemer, helps us, for He is the way, the truth and the life. He strives to lead all of us to our Father, out of the wheel of reincarnation and into the light, yes, into the kingdom of light to our true, eternal homeland, to the starting point of our spiritual being. This spiritual being incarnated, burdened itself, entered into the cycle of reincarnation and is called at every moment by the great Spirit, the All-Love, Wisdom and Kindness to come out, out of this wheel of suffering, of fear, worry and illness, and go all the way to our true origin, to the Kingdom of God, which wants to blossom in each one of us.

May your heart open wide, wide for the life that is God in us!

Appendix

The Inner Path
Collective Volume
The Cosmic School of Life
The Evolution into the Cosmic Consciousness

Every person finds himself on a certain path through life. At some point the question comes up: Why am I here at all? What goals should or do I want to follow? How can I achieve lasting happiness, freedom and success in my life? Most people repress these questions and simply live from day to day – for their family, for success at work, for raising their standard of living, etc. But the soul longs for more and for something that is lasting. It senses that it is of divine origin and that the meaning of life consists of freeing oneself from the ballast of the all-too-human, in order to again find eternal happiness in God.

The main concern of Jesus of Nazareth, and the main task of the Spirit of the Christ of God through His prophetess for today, was and is to bring the Original Christian School of Life for becoming one with the Spirit of God in us. It offers all willing people inestimable help in getting to know themselves, in clearing up their sins and in connecting with the divine in them. This is a mystical path of evolution, on which the pilgrim to God opens his spiritual consciousness level by level, thus finding his way to a God-filled life.

1300 pp. hardbd., Order No. S 150 en, US$ 29.99
ISBN 1-890841-01-3

Inner Prayer
Heart Prayer, Soul Prayer,
Ether Prayer, Healing Prayer

"Prayer is devotion. The one who prays opens the circle of life in him. The one who prays rightly each day, from the heart, will also safeguard the inner peace, even in the midst of the greatest uproar. But it must be learned ..."

128 pp., hardbd., Order No. S 307 en, US$ 7.99
ISBN 1-890841-11-0

The Prophet

*The voice of truth,
the prophetess of God speaks into our time
The fundamental issues of our time
to think about and to serve in self-recognition*

All the editions of "The Prophet" listed on the previous page are available free of charge, as well as our complete catalog of books, cassettes and videos and information about our radio programs.

Contact:

Verlag DAS WORT GmbH
Max-Braun-Str. 2
97828 Marktheidenfeld
Germany
Tel. + 49-9391-504-135
Fax + 49-9391-504-133

Gabriele Publishing House
P.O. Box 2221, Deering, NH 03244
(844) 576-0937
WhatsApp/Messenger: +49 151 1883 874
www.Gabriele-Publishing-House.com

Website: http/www.universal-spirit.cc
E-mail: info@das-wort.com